These are Frank Hildebrandt's words written over many years starting around the early '70's. Words and thoughts about the passing days of what came to his mind. They aren't in any special order, just inside for seeing the many years he felt at any given moment of time. Words sometimes on scraps of paper or a cocktail napkin. Saved for sharing to anyone's reading.
Some are written from his yearly Christmas cards sent to people that he has known over the years.
These may be his last writings!

Thoughts Along The Way

Frank Hildebrandt

Thoughts Along The Way

Copyright © 2025

All Rights Reserved

ISBN:

About the Author

For 46+ years, I've had a career in Law Enforcement. A dream I had since I was a little kid. Dreams sometimes do come true. Now that I am retired, I thought perhaps it was time to share these writings. So much time has passed. Most were written for someone special; shared, but most times not. Private thoughts that touched or were felt by me. Some did get shared, most not. Words were written down, hidden with some still sad. Most times, forgotten and filed away.

Never really forgotten.

Thoughts Along The Way

UNTITLED

May every door ahead,

open as you go.

And the ones you've

passed - stay ajar.

If for no other reason,

then to look back –

While always going on.

UNTITLED

Words that never

    will be spoken.

Are sounds that

    never will be heard.

Letters that never

    will be written.

Are thoughts that

    never will be read.

UNTITLED

There is a time for laughter,

        and there is a time for tears,

for each of us has happy days,

        and days when grief appears.

But we have our troubles,

        just as when we're glad and gay,

we should always remember,

        that this, too, will pass away.

Thoughts Along The Way

THE "GG" TRAIN (QUEENS OF BROOKLYN)

The ride
was longer than usual.
I felt it would last,
beyond the time
I had remaining.
To be late,
the excuse
couldn't be told.

Lights flash by.
It's late. No,
the sun hasn't risen.

I'm alone
this morning.
I felt it when I left.
My head still filled

there's nothing inside.

LOOK BACK

Sometimes,
  as we pass
    through this life
   a person catches
     a passing smile
       as we move by.

Thoughts are exchanged,
  then passed back.
As they entangle
  the closeness becomes
      apparent

    But, life
      with a pace that
  cannot stand still
    allows each person

Thoughts Along The Way

                    many paths.

  Roads to nowhere, yet
        ever moving to somewhere.
And yes,
      sometimes back to
            the beginning...

the smile.

Thoughts Along The Way

August 1985

HER EYES

W hen I look

    and see you

        looking,

your eyes show me

    something unique

        for the first time.

Perhaps, it's the

        way you're able

    to let me know

the feelings enclosed.

Maybe it's not intended

    to show feeling

        to me,

but

Thoughts Along The Way

        I hope to

    grasp the glance,

even for that
            brief second.

Please look back.

I never looked

    away.

Thoughts Along The Way

August 1985

THE ESCAPE

An affair
>is something
>>I use
>for the journey.

The journey
>which I have
taken before,
>>and
>returned alone.

Unsure,
>I need the thought
>>you're coming.

Don't ask,
>I don't know the course.

What I purpose

Thoughts Along The Way

        is uncertainty

               that

  I'll ever escape.

Let's draw a map.

Thoughts Along The Way

February 1987

THE WEEKEND

Did I say

    thank you?

It seems

    we steal,

for the weekends

    from a week

        of lost treasures.

We take each

    others dreams

        into a single

            move.

Moving forward

    in the discovery

of the end — and

Thoughts Along The Way

beginning of the

    search

        through

another week,

        for a glimpse

of the thought

        a weekend,

will come

        again....

And again.

UNTITLED

I'm in love

      with a dream.

Not so much

          with you,

    as the thought

        of you.

I know it's not love

but, I grasp for

        the dreams

    of a man in love.

Not with love.

I'll always dream,

    of you.

UNTITLED

A year passes
    with a bunk
        of an eye.

Only by
    keeping them
        open,
can I slow time.

I just haven't learned,
    to dream with
        open eyes.

UNTITLED

A‍s I pass AMCH

    her memory is

           felt.

I know she

        wasn't always mine

    but, there was

        a time I thought

            she was.

Deep inside me her

    love is there.

Now as I walk

              by,

    thinking only of

        the many times

Thoughts Along The Way

    I was here.

In my memories,

    she will

        always be mine.

I now share her,

    with no one.

UNTITLED

W hen,
    I try to talk
        with my feelings,
you never understand.
Do I expect
        too much
    from a relationship
           with you?
I'm trying
        to be more open,
    than you're
           able to accept.
Maybe,
    maybe not.
I took you
        as a precious stone.

MY BIRTHDAY

Next year

      I'll spend it different.

Only each year

has become

      a repeat,

           of the ones past.

 Next year,

I'll spend it different.

Thoughts Along The Way

March 1989

YOU MY FRIEND

Some people

    come into

        our lives

and leave,

    leaving us with

        many memories.

You my friend,

        have

    left me

        much to remember.

Memories,

    which tomorrow

        we can

remember…..

        You and I.

Thoughts Along The Way

YESTERDAY GONE BY

Yesterday's belong

    to one's past.

You can go back,

    but you cannot

    live ---

        time gone by.

Use your dreams

    to relive your memories

of the days

    that have gone

        by.

Life is meant

    to be lived for today

which is to become,

        tomorrow.

GIRAFFES

Giraffes are able

    to reach much

higher than I.

    Unlike the

  giraffes, I didn't understand

the extent of my reach.

I respect that, but

  don't understand

      why .....

Thoughts Along The Way

THE AIRPORT

Moving through

      the airport

I feel alone.

People rush to

      lines, few smile

only to wait.

Planes come

      and go.

New people rush

      by. All

going somewhere. Some

      going nowhere.

What seems

      to be the same?

As we fly

Thoughts Along The Way

from this place

    to that.

I had a plan

    or thought.

We expect and

    surely know

        no such plan

will always follow through.

I had a plan,

    what happened?

THE PASSING OF A DAISY

Now it's winter.

Cold, silent, lonely -----

   as I look out

      into the fields,

  snow covers the ground.

As sure as spring rains

     she will be back.

Reaching higher,

   greener than blades

      of grass.

Grasping the yellow

     in the golden sun ----

  she will still retain,

      the white of

   winter's edge.

Thoughts Along The Way

Calling to her

       now,

            through

the howling winter

       winds.

She will not respond

    to my voice.

She follows

    not me,

  she is too gentle

to fight the wind.

       But,

Spring is near.

The rain will replace

    the snow,

  the wind will pass.

  Passing on winter

to spring,

        she will come.

The sun will lift

        her into the air.

Drops of rain warmed

    by the sun, moves

    her into life.

Each day a little closer

    yet, nearer to

        when she will go.

The rains have stopped

    and the suns light,

   lets me see her.

Summer is the time

    she enjoys most.

      Watching her beauty now

          is hard to hold.

If I grasp her gentle

    frame, she will die.

But, leaving her there

        winter will again take

           her away.

Summer must give way

      to Fall.

Should I let her fade

   into the winter wind,

      or

         take hold

now, and hope?

Maybe

    if I gave her love

        she would not die.

The winter will take

    her back.

I'll reach out

  again

    for her.

If the winter takes her

  before I reach the fields,

    she will be gone.

Maybe she will come again

        and again

But, somehow I think -----

    this **Daisy**, may not.

The fields are

    within sight.

Thoughts Along The Way

Feeling chilled,

    my heart now subtle

  by the coming wind

      that winter always

           brings.

Just this once,

    couldn't winter

be late….

UNTITLED

Now,

for the second time

I find myself alone.

Alone in a time

when a man needs

a warm hand, a

tender touch, understanding,

but most of all

love.

Man can not

exist without it,

nor should he try.

I look within every woman,

but never find the

complete person I want.

Could it be I ----- who
must change.
Some have said yes,
many have said no.
I think not.

I want what is felt.
It's the feeling that
is not right..

I could give, if----
only you were right.

I will keep looking,
but how long will it take?
Maybe that question is
 incorrect or words wrong.

Thoughts Along The Way

I know time as a measurement

does not apply----I have

to put it another

way.

Which way?

UNTITLED

For each day we live

there will have been

    a yesterday.

Remember each day vividly

   forgetting

      not the smallest detail.

Don't allow the

   tomorrow's ahead----

To be empty of dreams

     of the days gone by.

THE LETTER THAT NEVER CAME

I waited for your letter.

No, it hasn't come

yet ---- maybe tomorrow.

She will surely send

a Christmas card ---- she's

good that way you know.

DISCARDED TREASURES

Walking along the beach

    I see how life

        moves along

the water's edge.

Washing in upon

    the shore

   then out ---- leaving

        treasures to be found,

discarded by the sea.

Some are again reclaimed

        and lost,

   most again

      discarded by the sea.

Treasures for those of us

        who seek them

to be saved in another

        corner of our world.

Only later

        to be discarded

and just maybe .....

            again reclaimed.

UNTITLED

Sadness never seems
    to totally end
   these last few years.

I must put together
         my life
  to reach a
    point of living.

The thought of
  giving up, is
    considered more often.

What sanity I still possess
  keeps me moving.
If that little bit

was to be drained

        now ----

The struggle would

    be over.

UNTITLED

As I am

    greeted by the

        sun

the desire for

        living becomes

    more evident.

If only the

        sun could shine,

    everyday.

WINDY NIGHT

As I sit,

    passing time

        with the wind,

the night brings

    moments of loneliness.

The feeling felt,

    when you move from

        my eyes.

I look for you

  and know you're safe,

    but not within my

        reach.

You're like the wind.

Thoughts Along The Way

Moving away, then back.

When you're near

    the warmth holds

           me within your arms.

 As you let go

    the wind returns --

let go as you must

    but, come back to me

         before the night

    gives way.

UNTITLED

I have chosen

    my profession....

You have trained

    me well....

We have given

    our best....

Now dear lord

    give me rest.

UNTILTED

Moments are

no longer moments.

They've come

together and

now---years

have passed.

Time builds

more distance,

then miles could

ever hope to do.

We can not move

back in time,

but miles can

be overcome.

Thoughts Along The Way

Run this way----

and hope.

Thoughts Along The Way

UNTITLED

My life

    seems to reach

        for more

            then I can find.

Why ----

    after all these

        years,

      haven't I been

    able to settle?

It's as if

    I am lost,

somewhere between

    yesterday and today.

Tomorrow will have

to bring the answer,

or the end.

UNTITLED

How do you say

to someone,

"I am losing you"?

Or perhaps

that's wrong, because

I have lost you.

Maybe not to him

or even the one

before that.

It's

more likely to be,

the one tomorrow.

And that,

not even I can stop

nor you.

But that lost,

if even recovered,

would never belong----

To me.

LAST NIGHT

Last night
    wasn't easy,
and this morning
    was even worse.

Tomorrow morning
    hasn't come,
maybe it will stay away
    just this once.

UNTITLED

You remember the dreams
          I had that first
    day we met?

They say
      it's good to dream you know.

I'm not so sure,
      sometimes they're just
           Dreams.

UNTITLED

Loneliness
>of unbearable magnitude
>>has entered my life.

Far greater then
>even I
>>had anticipated,
>or
knew possible.

Now,
>unable to deal
>>with it,
>I must act.

I find myself lost.
Never have I

seen life,

so empty.

Thoughts Along The Way

January 1978

THE SUN .... IS SHE

The sun
    seems to give way
to allow me
      another day.

I think back
    wondering why,
the last moments
      moved by so rapidly?

Then it's over.

It's recaptured,
        loved
again

lost to the night.

Now,

    with a mere blink

  of my eyes

    my memories

        hold

           the sun.

If only

    for that once,

  why couldn't….

          No.

Like the sun

    she

  will always come

    and will always go.

Thoughts Along The Way

Tomorrow

    I know the sun

        will come again.

Thoughts Along The Way

THE TORTOISE AND THE LADY

Life, comes and goes.

Each day passes

with time moving,

unable to slow

to my pace.

I have not known

the speed of others.

My motion slow,

as I wander with

the journey of time.

Somehow in the journey

the nearness of others,

a stranger to me.

Upon my shoulders

I struggle, with the

burden of my life.

Thoughts Along The Way

It's not easy

traveling slowly and alone.

She must have needed

a place to rest,

and I, her touch.

Now she, no added

burden to my life.

Rides with me,

through the journey

 of time.

UNTITLED

Listen,

    I'm here.

    Don't leave me yet.

        Where do I go?

        How do I pay?

Thoughts Along The Way

1977

SHE DOESN'T KNOW

W ho is he?

I can't make him go,
nor let him stay.

I can't put him down,
nor pick him up.

Yet,
why is he here?

I should know.
He knows.

Why not me?
Frank why?

UNTITLED

I plea for life

for death is close.

I can see it

yet, I can't look.

It's felt by me.

But, yet untouched.

It's here ---- next to me.

My breath short.

Darkness fills my eyes,

I no longer see.

My hand motionless

it's ended.

I'm dead.

UNTITLED

If man -----

Was to stop,

life is said to end.

UNTITLED

Listen to the sounds.

It's like you can feel

the chill, and

not merely the wind.

UNTITLED

I look back

at life

one could say,

to remember.

Life is made

of memories.

What was past

and what will pass.

Today somehow

leaves me to believe,

that my memories

lie within that past.

THE APARTMENT

Days have passed

since I was there.

I drove by today

only to remember yesterday,

or was it

the day before?

Time passes and we forget

somehow I remember.

Everyone sees the sign

"Apartment for Rent."

I was there, but

then so was she

at **255**.

Thoughts Along The Way

UNTITLED

As sure as the sun

      comes up each

   morning,

another day will

   get a new

        beginning.

YOU AND I ARE DIFFERENT.

It's hard to believe..

I'm not sure why

I guess,   no.

Maybe I'm different.

I would think

if only people would look.

You must be different.

To be the same

you see nothing,

outside your vision.

I want to see

beyond the farthest mountain.

To use only one's eyes

you lack the difference,

between you and I.

UNTITLED

As I find myself
    sad and lonely,
I just think
    about the days
        gone by.

I possess
    the power
  to recall all
    my yesterdays.
Reliving them
    one by one
  in my mind.

The reason is
    we are alive.
  And there will always

Thoughts Along The Way

be a tomorrow.

So today,

   will become a yesterday

      that can be remembered,

         or

just forgotten.

But never forget -----

There will always

     be memories,

   of the tomorrow's ahead.

UNTITLED

Today, as yesterday

will never be reclaimed.

For once something

is gone

this perhaps, is

when we must find

something in its place.

Love too becomes

lost, but we somehow

someway replace that.

But, in the replacement

what was passed

is still there.

For-----

Love that is received

is never truly forgotten!

UNTITLED

If,

I was to touch

you again.

I'm sure it would

be the same.

Remembering --- the parts

that were made

to be touched.

And the parts,

made only to be

held---

The handle bars ---------

UNTITLED

Sometimes,

there comes a time

when people need.

And, with each need

want someone. And

with this want,

which may come

at any time.

Seems to come

at the end,

Christmas is said

to come at the

end,

of December.

So this Christmas,

I need and want

you.

I'm people----

UNTITLED

A birthday---

Which comes once

in any given year.

Is never remembered

by many, other

than the person

forgotten.

More than not,

it is remembered.

But,

not at the right time.

So I send this card today

for the many

Happy Birthday's of

yesterday----

SEEDS

If we were

to collect -----

A few seeds everyday,

and save them

until it rains.

On that day,

we could start

from the beginning.

Each seed has

the power of life.

So life can start

when we begin.

UNTITLED

I find it hard

to remember.

Not of you,

which is something

that can't be

forgotten. But ------

Of the last time

we touched.

It seems to be

such a long time ago -----

THE LOSS OF A DAISY

I passed by the field
        and thought of you.
Never have I seen
        so many before.

Could I hold
        the beauty I could see?

As I made my way
        I wanted to grasp
    each and every one.

I tried as you see,
        but
none are mine.

Take what I have
seen. They are yours.

Thoughts Along The Way

I remember

    each time I pass,

but a single one.

    Or by just

        thinking of you.

UNTITLED

As I find myself
> sad and lonely,

I just think
about the days
> gone by.

I possess
the power
to recall all
> my yesterdays.

Reliving them
one by one
in my mind.

The reason is
we are alive.
And there will always

Thoughts Along The Way

       be a tomorrow.

So today,

   will become a yesterday

      that can be remembered

         or

just forgotten.

But never forget---

There will always

    be memories,

of the tomorrows ahead.

Thoughts Along The Way

January 31, 2006

WHERE HAVE THE FLOWÉRS GONE?

The Flowérs

    have come

        and gone…

We had, but

    a short time

        to watch them grow.

I got to know,

    her smile

  for too short

        of time.

No one knows

    just how long

Thoughts Along The Way

Flowérs will

grow.

Perhaps if we

let them go

wild

on their own,

they could survive.

No one knows

just how long

Flowérs will

grow.

I had thought

that,

that this Flowér

won't die.

She gave me

so much joy,

   in the colors

      of her

         smile.

"… do you know

     how much I love

         you?..." seemed

   to be

what echoed from

     her smile.

How did the

   sunshine

leave us so soon?

No one knows

   just how long

      Flowérs will

         grow.

Thoughts Along The Way

For my wife,

Marléne Michael who

was always my Flowérs

Thoughts Along The Way

CONTENTS:

1985: It's cold, and Christmas

1985: Glimpse of Christmas past

1986: The night before

1986: Christmas revealed

1988: Christmas magic

1990: For yet another year

1991: Searching at Christmas

1994: A gift for Christmas

1994: Christmas back then

1995: Christmas lights

1998: Toys **R** us

1998: Changing colors

1999: Ice crystals

2002: The wreath on the door

2003: The Christmas card

2004: The creek

Thoughts Along The Way

1985

IT'S COLD, AND CHRISTMAS

The snow has

    started

  and the night has come,

lying across the sky

      as a cold blanket.

I feel chilled,

    seeing the wind

   blow the snow against

      my window.

Looking out into the

    winter's night

  I think of so many

     moments...

   yet past,

Thoughts Along The Way

and some that

I hope to come.

It's Christmas,

and the snow

is most welcome tonight.

People are locked inside

with friends,

loves and loves that might

have been,

but never will.

I dream upon

each snowflake

and watch them disappear

within the night sky,

only to be rebuilt

upon the ground.

Thoughts Along The Way

I now drift,

    as with the snow.

  Drift as we may tonight

      upon the snow

in front of our eyes

      memories fade,

  blending amidst the snow

      then only to be set

        adrift,

    by the wind.

Behind my window

    the wind reminds me

      it's cold, and Christmas.

People are locked inside

      with friends,

  loves and loves that might

      have been,

Thoughts Along The Way

but never will.

1985

GLIMPSE OF CHRISTMAS PAST

T he ground is

    covered with

        snow.

  As I walk and

      remember

  years back,

Christmas was so

    much different

        back then.

Windows are dressed

    with lights blinking

        a warm welcome

  as I pass by.

  Inside one catches

Thoughts Along The Way

    a glimpse of faces,

        smiles and friends.

As I stand

    staring,

I feel warm

    as the wind blows

        against my face.

It's cold,

    and as the snow

        falls,

I'm reminded I must

    move on.

Down the road

    home waits,

        and it's Christmas.

Thoughts Along The Way

Thoughts Along The Way

1986

THE NIGHT BEFORE

The sun
> moves down

making way for the
> evening stars.

The night is chilled,
> with
> the light snow

that falls upon my
> face.

The rush of people
> leaving the
> > stores,

> pushing past

with the last

minute treasures.

As I walk,

    the familiar bell

        is ringing.

The little woman dressed

    in red

requesting a bit of

        sharing,

that comes with Christmas.

The snow is a little

    heavier now,

as it builds under

        each step.

    A little closer to

        home,

where one will find

    the outstretched arms

Thoughts Along The Way

of friends and loves

    we will share,

  this Christmas

    season with.

Thoughts Along The Way

1986

CHRISTMAS REVEALED

As I sit,

   my eyes

      once again

   gaze into the

         fireplace.

I ponder,

    as I watch

  the fire flicker.

The familiar smells

      of Christmas

   fill the air.

Slowly drifting,

Thoughts Along The Way

I imagine
> the thoughts
of Christmas morning.

Packages being opened,
> the anticipation of
>> discovering dreams,
> the disappointment of
>> forgotten hopes.

Thinking back,
> thoughts
>> of so many years
>>> drift past.

As the fire crackles,
> I'm brought
>> back.

Tomorrow is Christmas.
> And

so come the dreams

        and hopes

  we will discover,

this Christmas season.

1988

CHRISTMAS MAGIC

A̲s I turned
 another page,
  drifting
 the book
  I held
   felt heavy,
as I
 was
  made
 warm by
  the
   fire.

My mind turned
 from the printed pages,

Thoughts Along The Way

    to the thoughts
        of Christmas.

Christmas for most,
        had started.

Not much like
    years ago,
  when we thought
      Santa Claus brought
        the MAGIC,
the boxes under
        the trees,
  and the joy
        in people's hearts.

I guess I fell
    asleep
in this old soft chair.
        But,

Thoughts Along The Way

    I seem to remember

  the lights on the

        tree were out.

    And those gifts---

As I looked up

  rubbing my eyes,

    I saw her smiling.

"It's MAGIC," she said

  with a smile

    and a ho ho ho.

I knew then,

  as long as

    one believes,

  Christmas is the MAGIC

    within all of

      us.

Thoughts Along The Way

1990

FOR YET ANOTHER YEAR

The smell of
> pine has faded
> for yet another year.

The holidays have passed,
> and we remember
> the excitement which was
>> built into a
> single morning.

Perhaps it's good Christmas
> comes but once a year.
>> Leaving us with
> undisappointed dreams
> lasting throughout the year.

Thoughts Along The Way

Oh yes, just as we

        move through

    the months until the

          magic comes back,

    we shall not forget.

The reminders are found,

    rediscovered, lost

  within the many corners

of our lives.

The glimmer is unmistaken.

That piece of tinsel

    curled in that corner,

        overlooked, forgotten.

Tucked away with those

    undisappointed dreams.

And,

    left in place

        for yet another year.

Thoughts Along The Way

1991

SEARCHING AT CHRISTMAS

W here was it that

   we went

      in search of a tree?

I remember that walk

   so long ago.

The December air hinted

      that Christmas was near.

The cold wasn't felt then,

     only the thoughts

        of Christmas.

We made our way

   and somehow knew,

Thoughts Along The Way

  which one to cut.

Does it always happen
  that way?

That tree was long ago
   discarded,
  that Christmas
    has passed years of others,
 and now,
   to another…

We no longer walk
   through those woods
  in search of a tree.

We found it that year.

I guess I did discover
   many things then.

Thoughts Along The Way

Just what they were

    are now left to memories.

I wonder if people

    still do that,

  search for a tree?

1994

A GIFT FOR CHRISTMAS

In and out
> of the stores,
>
> we search
>> to discover the joy,
>>
>> that one special offering
>>> to share with another
>>>
>>>> and another.

What is it,
> that makes us search endlessly
>> until we find it?
>>
>> Do we ever find
>>> that special gift
>>>> of sharing?

Thoughts Along The Way

Maybe it's really out

        in the open.

Perhaps inside our thoughts

        or

wrapped within

        our hearts.

Gifts at Christmas

    are not always within paper.

        To be unwrapped with hands

            paper discarded.

    Most times,

they're stored within us.

    Shared,

given away

    and maybe taken back.

The real gifts

    at Christmas

are always within us.

Passed with a mere glance,

   a spoken word,

      a smile.

It's not for sale,

   held or

      unwrapped.

It's felt between us.

1994

CHRISTMAS BACK THEN

It's not yet morning,

    it's dark,

  the light hasn't crept in

        between the curtain

           openings.

The windows always seemed

      to have had frost on them.

          I remember our windows

             had shades.

    Did they have window blinds

          back then?

My brother slept

    below me

on the lower bunk.

    My sister

  in the other room,

    no others.

They came later,

  my little brother

      and sister.

None of that mattered

    back then

  not even the cold

    linoleum floors.

      Did everyone

  have linoleum?

It was okay then

  to get up early

    or

  at least

we were not scolded for long.

Thoughts Along The Way

Christmas came

    and went back then

  as it does for most kids.

Searching through

    my mind,

I can't remember much more

      about those mornings---

  Rice Krispies and milk

and my feet

    on the cold linoleum floors.

Thoughts Along The Way

1995

CHRISTMAS LIGHTS

The leaves
>aren't quite covered
>>yet.

The colors still
>shine
>>through
>the snow,
>>almost
>melting the flakes
>>as they fall.

The cold and wind
>have stayed away,
>>the snow

Thoughts Along The Way

    tries to build

           a blanket

      to hide

    what the trees gave away.

    We always wish

           for the snow

      this day, but

    I'm glad the leaves

           won.

    The colors feel

      so much warmer

           now,

      more like lights

    glimmering among the trees.

Thoughts Along The Way

Thoughts Along The Way

1998

TOYS R US

Do you really

        think

      Christmas is about

        toys?

I think I thought
   that. At least
at one time I did.

I learned
   the true meaning
      of Christmas,
   way back then.
I mean I know,
   but the toys

Thoughts Along The Way

were Christmas.

I haven't received
> any toys in many years,

I don't even believe
> I still have any.

Does someone
> give them back
>> or, do they just
>>> disappear?

I wouldn't want that---
> you know,

the disappearing part.

I guess I should
> just believe that

Christmas is magic.

Thoughts Along The Way

The magic that comes

      and goes within us.

  It doesn't need

        to be real,

    imaginary

        or even seen.

Just as long as you—

    believe.

Never let it disappear

    no matter where

        the toys **R**.

Thoughts Along The Way

Thoughts Along The Way

1998

CHANGING COLORS

Walking,

    the leaves crunch

        under the weight

            of my feet.

    The sounds,

    we've grown to know.

On this clear day,

    as the bright sun

        shines through

    the trees,

the reds, yellows, oranges, greens

    color my thoughts.

For sure,

Thoughts Along The Way

winter
    lies ahead.

The leaves will
    give way
and the snow
    will fall.

The shy has changed
    and the blowing wind,
has moved the colors
        behind doors.

Inside, the trees
    are green
covered by the color
        of lights and dreams.
They replace the fallen
    leaves
        reds, yellows, oranges…

Thoughts Along The Way

I'll miss the fall,

    as I always do.

        But,

            it gives us

    the winter.

Passing into spring,

    with a short

    stop at Christmas.

A brief moment in time,

    between the

        changing colors.

1999

ICE CRYSTALS

The rains have
        slowed,
    to that faint drizzle
        my face
can't escape.

The cold holds the drops
    that freeze, building
as they land
        on the ground.

The snow becomes entombed
    with no escape. Covered,
        guarded, protected
by the frozen mist.

Ice Crystals crack

        under my very

                steps.

As the sun's

        light struggles,

    stealing the sky…

The ice won.

Covered,

    the glitter takes over

        once the rain

                passes.

For the moment,

    we succumb in awe,

        to the **"Ice Crystals."**

Thoughts Along The Way

Thoughts Along The Way

2002

THE WREATH ON THE DOOR

The smell in

    the air,

  is just about gone.

Needles

    have already started

        falling.

Opening the door,

    the wind blowing

  dropping them to my feet.

Weeks ago,

    the smell came

        back

  I looked for that hook

Thoughts Along The Way

    realizing,

there never was.

A way is found,

    captured

        but,

a promise never kept.

Each year,

    meaning to get something,

        planning

          and

each year waiting

    for the next.

The smell again

    will return.

Needles fall

    as the wind blows

        in the open door.

Each year,

    looking to the next…

As the door is closed,

        the smell is gone.

2003

THE CHRISTMAS CARD

Little snow
 is forecasted,
  as I walk
 to the box.

Most days,
  this time
   of year,
 it's easy to be
   reminded
  of friends,
   family
 and so much more.

You sort through

Thoughts Along The Way

    the pile

        you hold

    looking, reading

        and

            figuring out

    those return addresses.

Who sent them,

    who remembered,

        who didn't,

and those that

    couldn't, but

        you remember.

The cards are

    the way we

        remember,

    and will remember

        and remember…

Thoughts Along The Way

2004

THE CREEK

Earlier today

   the sounds

      could be heard.

Water running

        as it flows

   over the rocks.

The snow from the trees

      dropping in clumps,

  melting,

     adding to the sounds.

The creek is usually

   frozen by 'Christmas'

Thoughts Along The Way

    most years.

Sounds heard

    at winter's end.

A tree had fallen

    from winters back.

The weight

    of a storm,

        long past.

They say

    the cold weather

        isn't

            far away.

Perhaps!

Tomorrow

    the creek

Thoughts Along The Way

   will slow again,

       freeze…

   and 'Christmas' comes,

       the day after that.

Thoughts Along The Way

Thoughts Along The Way

I GUESS WE
JUST CONTINUE
DOWN THE ROAD.
HOPE YOU ENJOYED
THE BOOK.
    FRANK

Thoughts Along The Way

www.ingramcontent.com/pod-product-compliance
Ingram Content Group UK Ltd.
Pitfield, Milton Keynes, MK11 3LW, UK
UKHW020239240426
12049UKWH00007B/129